STEP-BY-STEP

MAKING PRINTS

DERI ROBINS

ILLUSTRATED BY JIM ROBINS

Kingfisher Books

NEW YORK

KINGFISHER BOOKS,
Grisewood & Dempsey Inc.
95 Madison Avenue
New York, New York 10016

First American edition 1993
10 9 8 7 6 5 4 3 2 1 (lib.bdg.)
10 9 8 7 6 5 4 3 2 1 (pbk.)

Library of Congress Cataloging-
in-Publication Data
Robins, Deri.
   Making prints / Deri Robins.
   p.c. — (Step-by-step)
   Summary: Introduces
printmaking and features
instructions for such activities
as body printing, letterpress,
marbling, and fabric printing.
1. Prints — Technique — Juvenile
literature. [1. Prints — Technique.]
I. Title II. Series: Step-by-step
(Kingfisher Books)
NE855.R72 1993
760'.28 — dc20 92-40216 CIP AC

ISBN 1-85697-925-3 (lib.bdg.)
ISBN 1-85697-924-5 (pbk.)

Designed by Ben White
Illustrations by Jim Robins
Photography by Rolf Cornell,
Cover design by Terry Woodley

Printed in Hong Kong

CONTENTS

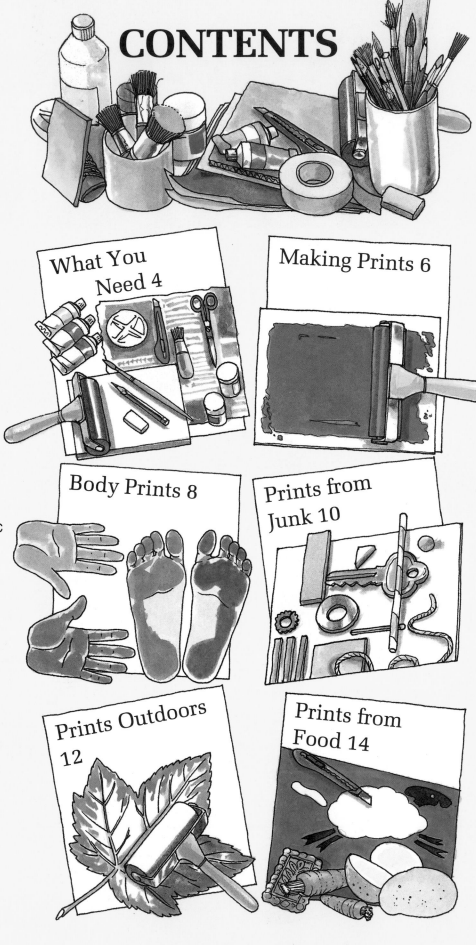

What You Need 4

Making Prints 6

Body Prints 8

Prints from Junk 10

Prints Outdoors 12

Prints from Food 14

Cardboard Prints 16

Letter Press 18

Print a Picture 20

Making Blocks 22

Scraper Prints 24

Monoprints 26

Stenciling 28

Marbling 32

Fabric Prints 34

China Prints 36

Using Prints 38

More Ideas 40

WHAT YOU NEED

Most of the prints shown in this book are made from ordinary bits and pieces from around the house. The only extra equipment you will need are brushes, a roller, plenty of paints, and a good supply of paper!

Printers

Look around the home (and the yard) for objects to print with — anything that has an interesting shape or texture will do.

Keep a junk box, and save useful things such as old cardboard boxes, string, broken toys, offcuts of wood, corks, etc.

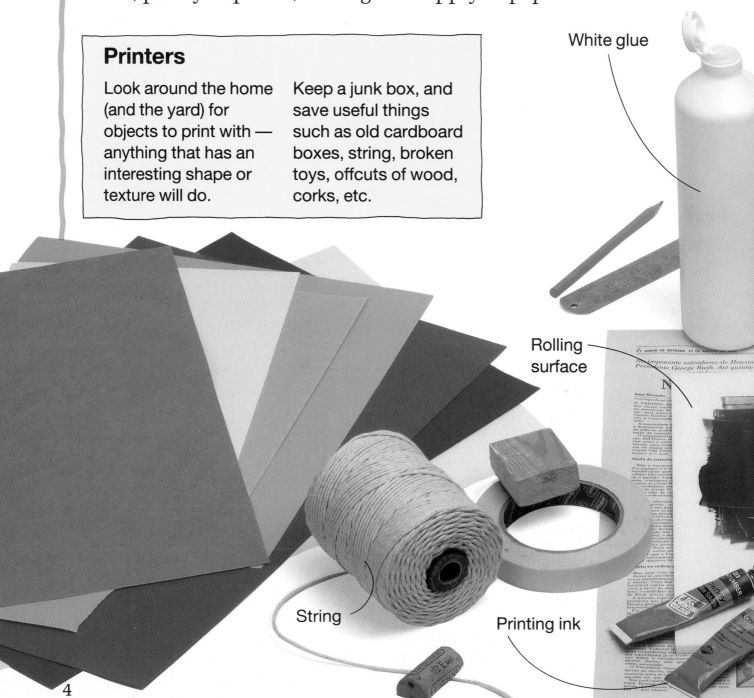

White glue

Rolling surface

String

Printing ink

Paints

Any thick paint can be used to make prints. Most of the prints in this book were made with printing inks — these can be bought from any art and craft shop. It's best to buy water-based inks, as these are the easiest and the cleanest to use. For marbling (see page 32) you will need some oil-based paint and mineral spirits. To print onto fabric and china (see page 34-37) you will need to buy special fabric and ceramic paints.

Tools of the Trade

For some of the prints in this book, you will need a roller and a large smooth surface such as a piece of formica.

For others, you will just need paint brushes and a saucer for mixing paints. You will also need some white glue, scissors, and an art knife. Finally, keep a supply of newspaper handy to protect your working area.

Cookie cutters

Fabric paint

Art knife

Ceramic paint

Glitter

Roller

MAKING PRINTS

This book shows you how to carry out many simple printing methods, from relief printing and stenciling to marbling and monoprinting. Before you start, read the hints and tips on these pages carefully.

SAFETY NOTE

To do some of the activities in this book, you will need to use an art knife. These are very sharp and can be dangerous unless used properly. Always make sure that an adult is around to help or supervise.

Printing Patterns

If you want to print a regular pattern, it is best to draw a grid on your printing area before you begin. Use a pencil, and erase the lines when the paint has dried completely.

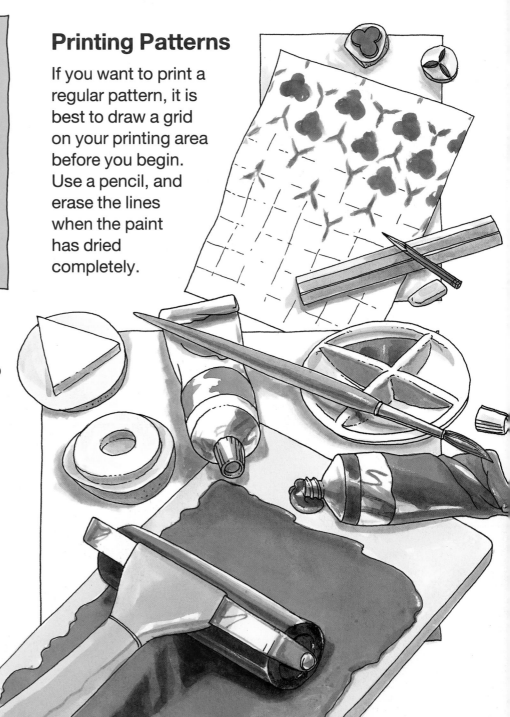

Applying Paint

Paint can be applied to a surface with either a brush or a roller — see which you find easier.

Rollers allow you to apply the paint quickly and evenly, but it can often be cheaper to squeeze out a small amount of paint and to apply it to your printer with a brush.

Mixing Prints

You can try overlapping different shapes and colors, as shown in the main picture. The flowers and leaves were cut from cardboard (see page 16), and the grid design was made with a plastic brick.

You can add the second layer when the first coat has dried, or when it is still wet — each method gives a different result. See which one you prefer.

Keep a sample of your most successful prints in a notebook or an album. You could also make a collage using scraps of printed paper.

Experiment with paper — brown paper, newspaper, and tissue all work well. You can also use white glue instead of paint — sprinkle with glitter while it is still wet.

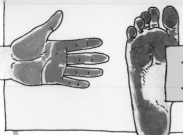

BODY PRINTS

In relief printing, an object is covered with paint or ink and then pressed down on paper. The simplest relief prints of all are those done with your fingers — or your thumbs, toes, or even your lips! Because body prints are so quick and easy, they make an ideal introduction to printing.

1

Mix your paint with a little water in a saucer. It should be thick and sticky, not runny.

2

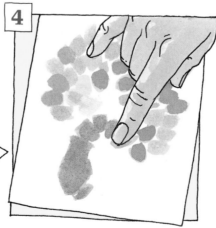

Roll the tips of your fingers from side to side in the ink. Press down on the paper.

3

Take a print of the fingers and thumbs of both your hands to make a complete fingerprint record.

4

Try building pictures from finger-and-thumb prints. Use the sides as well as the tips of your fingers.

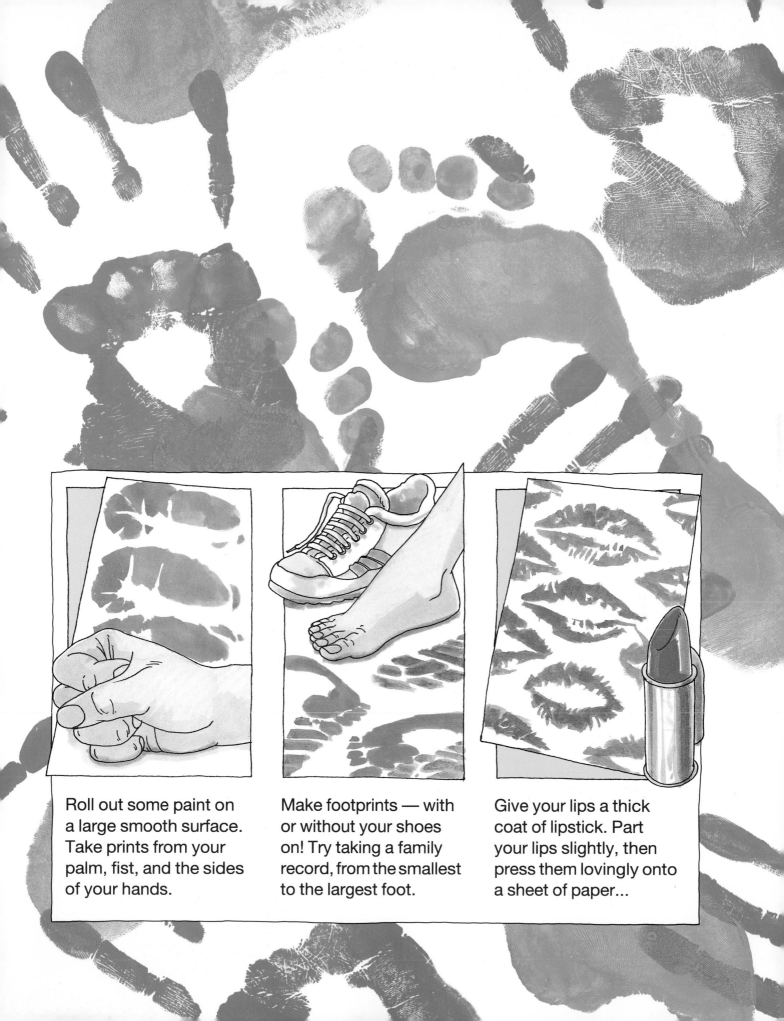

Roll out some paint on a large smooth surface. Take prints from your palm, fist, and the sides of your hands.

Make footprints — with or without your shoes on! Try taking a family record, from the smallest to the largest foot.

Give your lips a thick coat of lipstick. Part your lips slightly, then press them lovingly onto a sheet of paper...

PRINTS FROM JUNK

Take prints from broken toys, pieces of string, old keys, scrap pieces of wood — practically anything looks interesting if you repeat it often enough to make a pattern! Use junk to make relief prints, or try spattering with paint as shown opposite.

Below: These prints were made with the following (left to right): a piece of bubble-wrap; bits of old toys; a building block; a cork cut in half lengthwise.

Relief Prints

Use a brush to cover one side of your printer with paint. Press down on paper, and repeat to build up a pattern. The pattern can be random, or even and regular as shown here.

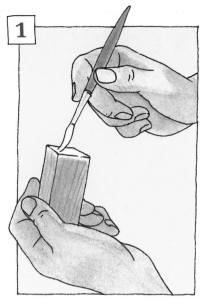

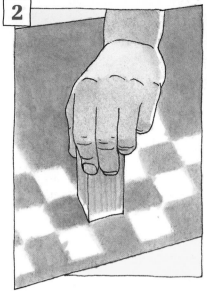

Spattering

Lay random items on a sheet of paper. Dip an old toothbrush in paint, and run your finger over the brush to spatter the paint toward the paper.

Move all of the objects slightly, and spatter with a second color.

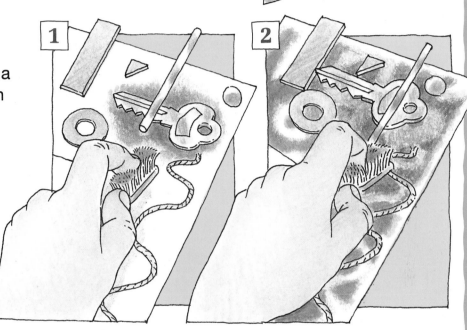

Mystery Print

Dip a piece of string in paint. Lay it on a sheet of paper, and put another sheet of paper on top. Press down, and pull the string out. Take off the top paper to reveal your mystery print!

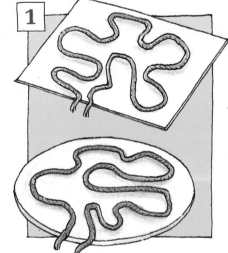

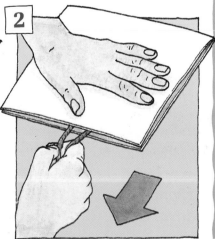

PRINTS OUTDOORS

When you've run out of household junk to print from, go and see what you can find in the yard! Leaves, twigs, bark, and ferns all make lovely natural shapes and patterns. Look out also for interesting "street furniture" such as old manhole covers — these can be used for taking rubbings.

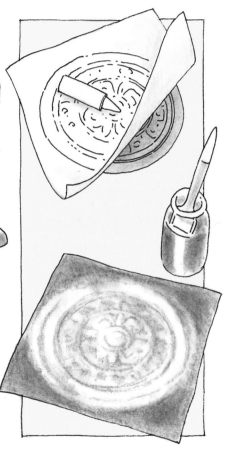

Leaf Prints

Using a brush or a roller, apply thick paint to the underside of a leaf. Lay it on a sheet of paper, and press down firmly.

Seashore Prints

Go beachcombing for interesting things to print with — try using driftwood, dried sea-weed, and shells of all shapes and sizes.

Rubbings

Use wax crayons to take rubbings from manhole covers or the bark of a tree. Brush the paper with thin paint — what happens?

Use a few different leaves to build up a regular pattern. Try overlapping the first leaves with the second and third ones once the paint has dried.

PRINTS FROM FOOD

Potatoes are perfect for making pictures — try cutting them into different shapes to build up a lively frieze like the one shown below. Check the fruit and vegetable rack for other useful printers — you should be able to come up with a huge variety of fascinating shapes and textures, but ask permission first.

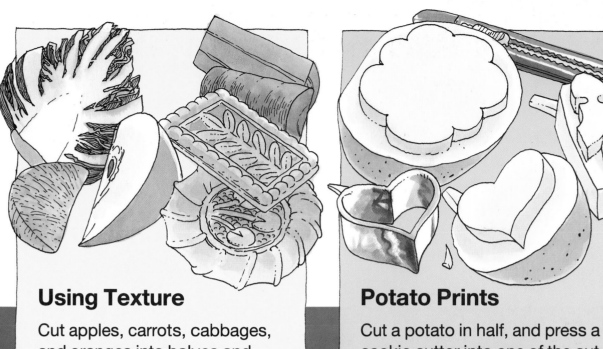

Using Texture

Cut apples, carrots, cabbages, and oranges into halves and segments. Dip them into a saucer of thick paint, and press down on paper. Dried pasta and cookies with raised surfaces also give good results.

Potato Prints

Cut a potato in half, and press a cookie cutter into one of the cut surfaces. Trim around the shape with a knife. Or make up your own shapes, and cut them out with the knife. Combine several shapes in one print, as below.

CARDBOARD PRINTS

Save pieces of cardboard — empty tubes, boxes, and packing material can all be used to make bright, colorful prints. Mix some fairly thick paint and spread it evenly on a plate. Press the pieces of cardboard into the paint and print.

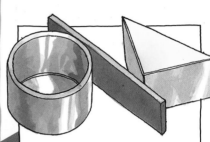

Using Edges

Use tubes to print circles — dip the edges into thick paint, or apply with a brush. Try using straight edges to make lines, or bend them into shapes and tape together.

Texture

Cut shapes from corrugated cardboard to make prints with a striped texture. Make simple handles by cutting strips of cardboard as shown, and gluing them to the backs.

Smooth Board

Cut pieces of thick, smooth cardboard into stars, circles, strips, flowers, and other shapes. To make the prints more interesting, cut holes out of the pieces of cardboard.

Below: Cardboard prints are perfect for making bright-colored wrapping paper — or, on a grander scale, for printing your own wallpaper!

Going Further

Cut two identical shapes from cardboard — for example, a tiger or a zebra. Cut out extra details, such as the zebra's stripes, and glue them onto one of the pieces.

Roll thick paint over the plain piece of cardboard, and press down to take a print. When it has dried, roll a darker color over the raised surface on the second piece of cardboard. Press it down over the first print.

LETTER PRESS

Cut big, bold letters and numbers out of cardboard — they're perfect for printing eye-catching posters, or your own personalized stationery. If you don't want to make a complete printing press, just cut out the letters or numbers you need.

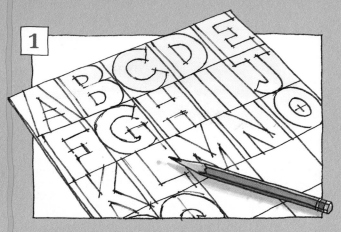

1 Divide a thick piece of cardboard into squares of equal size — about $\frac{3}{4}$ x 1 inch. Make a square for each letter or number you want to print.

2 Draw the letters and numbers in the squares, making them thick and block-like. Cut them out carefully with an art knife (ask an adult to help).

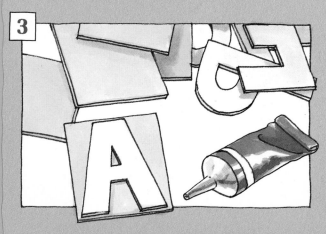

3 Cut another set of squares, the same size as the first. Glue the letters to the middle of the squares. Glue them on back to front, so that they will print the right way around.

4 Roll thick paint over the raised surface of the letters, and press down on paper to print. If you are printing a whole word or sentence, it helps to draw pencil lines first.

Name stamps

Instead of individual letter blocks, you may prefer to make a single block containing your name or initials.

Cut the letters you need from cardboard as before. Periods can be made with a hole punch.

Cut a strip of cardboard, as wide as the letters. Glue the letters in place, reading back to front.

PRINT A PICTURE

This cardboard printing press can be used to make your own special run of pictures or greeting cards. You will need to make a separate printing block for each color you use.

1 Make a color drawing. Cut a piece of tracing paper to fit the drawing, and trace the outlines with a soft pencil.

2 Cut four pieces of cardboard the same size as the tracing paper. Lay the tracing over one piece of cardboard.

3 Rub over all the outlines with a pencil, so that you have an exact copy of the drawing. Cut out all the shapes.

4 Tape the tracing to another piece of cardboard. Choose one color, and trace all the objects in that color.

5 Glue the shapes for that color to the outlines drawn on the cardboard. Do the same for the other two colors.

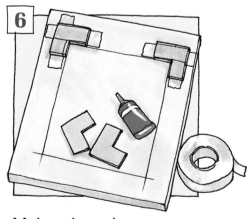

6 Make a base by drawing around one of the blocks. Tape down corners cut from cardboard.

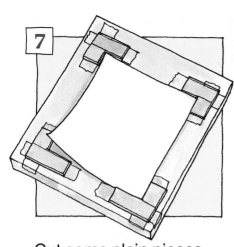

7

Cut some plain pieces of paper the same size as the printing blocks. Lay one sheet of paper between the corners.

8

Mix the paint so that it is ready to use. Roll paint over the raised surface of one of the printing blocks.

9

Using each of the colors in turn, press the printing blocks firmly down onto the same piece of paper.

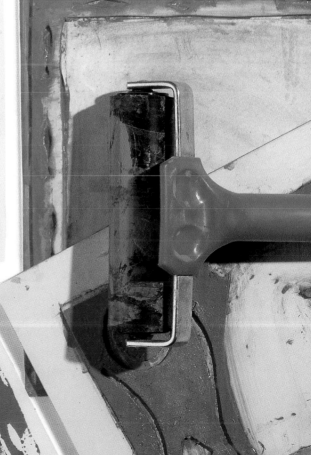

MAKING BLOCKS

Long-lasting printing blocks can be made by gluing objects or shapes to wood or thick cardboard. Add color and texture to your prints by using two or three blocks, as here. In addition to string and foam, you could try using matchsticks, buttons, coins, or dried spaghetti — the list is endless!

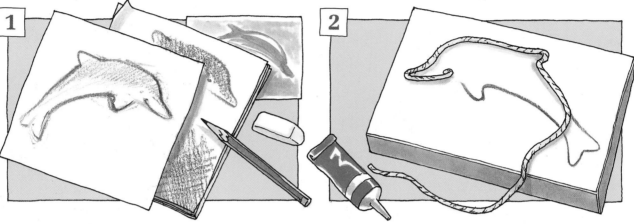

1 Make color sketches for the design you want to print. Trace the outline on thin cardboard, and cut it out to make a template.

2 Turn the template the wrong way around, and draw around the outline on a small piece of wood. Glue string to the outline.

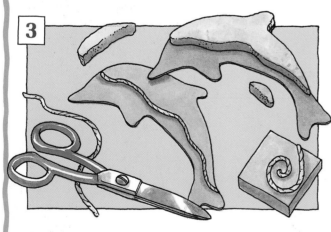

3 Cut two more templates from thick cardboard. Glue string and foam to the surface, as shown. The fourth block is made from wood and string.

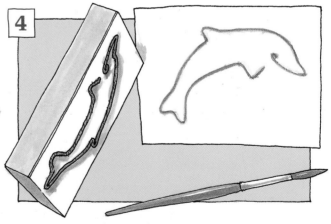

4 Roll paint over the blocks, and use them to make a number of prints. Add texture and color by overprinting with the two cardboard blocks.

For a tiled effect, cut out your prints and glue them to a large sheet of dark paper. Draw guidelines with a ruler and pencil first, to help you line the "tiles" up. You could even use your design to print real bathroom tiles (see page 36).

SCRAPER PRINTS

The secret of scraper printing is to keep the paint very thick and even, and to make the pattern quickly before the paint has a chance to dry. Scrape lines and swirls with pieces of cardboard — or draw a picture with a wooden stick.

1 Cut strips from thick cardboard, each 4 in. long. Cut different shapes along one edge.

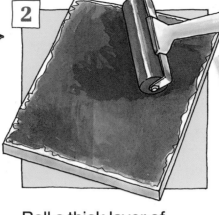

2 Roll a thick layer of paint or printing ink over a large, smooth surface.

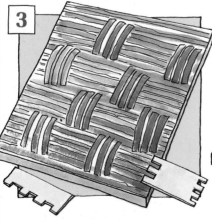

3 Use the strips of cardboard to scrape lines in the paint — they can be short or long, straight, wavy, or curved.

4 Lay a sheet of paper over the paint, and press firmly over the surface. Peel off the paper to see the print.

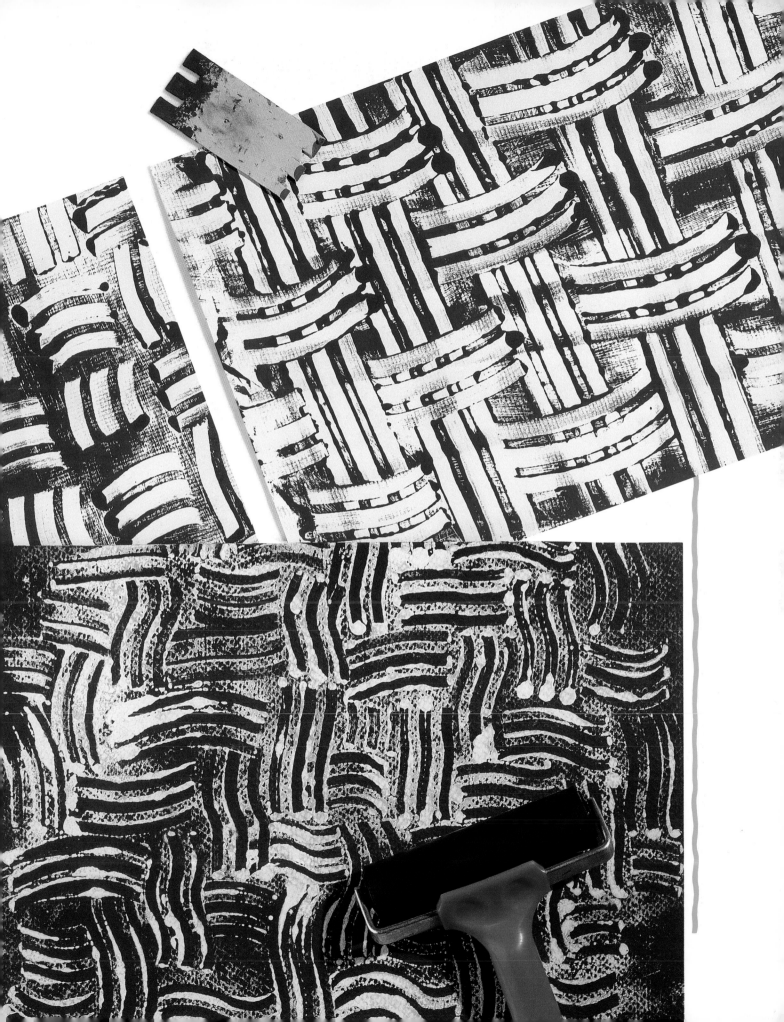

MONOPRINTS

A monoprint (literally, "one print") cannot be repeated — each one you make will be unique. As with scraper prints, you should take the print immediately, before the paint has a chance to dry.

26

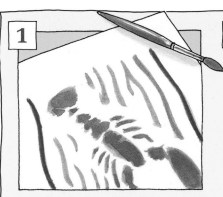

1 Paint a picture on a flat piece of formica or linoleum, using thick paint or printing ink. Keep the painting simple, and do it as quickly as possible.

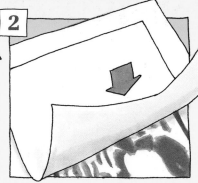

2 Lay a clean sheet of paper on top of the painting. Press down over the surface with your fingers, being careful not to smudge the paint underneath.

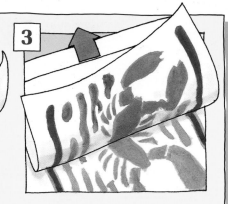

3 Peel the paper off the painted surface to see your print. The print should have a soft, slightly blurred texture, unlike a painting done with a brush.

STENCILING

The prints on these pages were all made with stenciling cards, but any thin cardboard would do. Ask an adult to help you cut out the shapes with an art knife, and use a thick stenciling brush to "stipple" on the paint using short, strong strokes.

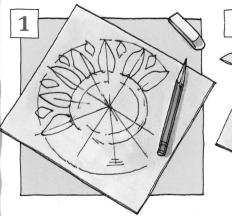

1

Draw a design on the cardboard with pencil. Try not to make the design too complicated.

2

Cut out with an art knife (ask an adult to help). Leave "bridges" between the holes.

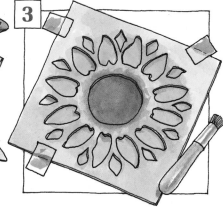

3

Tape the stencil to the paper, and stipple the paint through the holes with a stencil brush.

Doily Stencils

Make a doily by folding a square of paper in half several times. Snip holes from the folded edges, unfold the paper, and smooth out the creases.

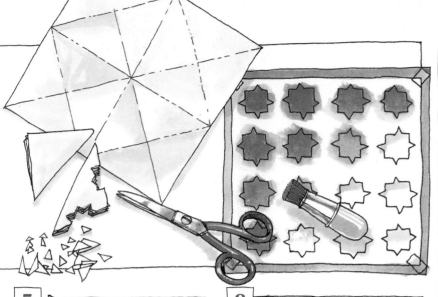

4

Before applying a second stencil, make sure that the paint from the first one has dried.

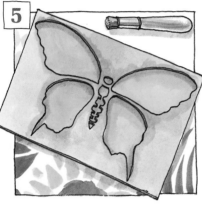

5

The butterfly was done in several stages. First, a stencil for the whole shape was used.

6

After the yellow paint had dried, two more stencils were used to print over the top.

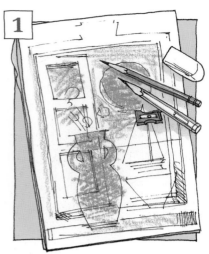

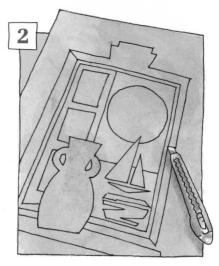

Using Masks

Sketch a design on a sheet of paper using colored pencils. Try to keep the design fairly simple, so that you can cut it out easily.

Trace your design onto stenciling cardboard, and cut out the shapes with an art knife. Lay them on a sheet of paper and fit them back together like a jigsaw.

Tape down the outer frame. Choosing one color at a time, take out all the pieces for that color and spray the spaces left behind. When dry, replace the shapes and repeat for the next color. Some areas (like the sea in our picture) could be sprayed with more than one color.

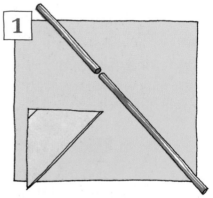

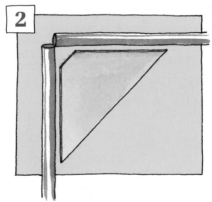

Make a Spray

Cut off the top third of a thin plastic straw. Cut a cardboard triangle and snip off the corner. Use this triangle to support the straws at a right angle, and use tape to hold all three pieces in place.

Fill a small dish with paint thinned with water. Dip the short end of the straw in the paint. Point the join at the paper, and blow gently from the other end.

Spraying paint is a messy business! Always surround your working area with lots of newspaper.

MARBLING

To make beautiful marbled papers, you will need some oil paints, mineral spirits, and a large shallow tray or bowl filled with water. As water and oil don't mix, the oil paint will float on top of the water and stick to the paper when you take a print.

1

Mix some oil paint with mineral spirits — the paint should be runny enough to fall in drips from the brush. Start with two different colors.

2

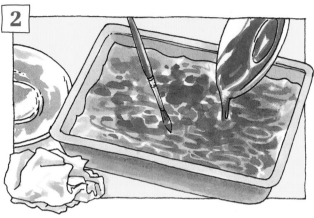

Use the brush to flick drops of paint over the water, or pour across the surface straight from the saucer. Swirl gently with the end of the brush.

3

Hold a sheet of paper by the opposite corners, and lay it gently over the surface. Smooth the surface to get rid of any air bubbles. The oil paint will cling to the paper.

4

Lift the paper off and leave to dry. Add more paint to make a second print. Try adding wallpaper paste before you add paint — this helps swirl the paint into a feathery pattern.

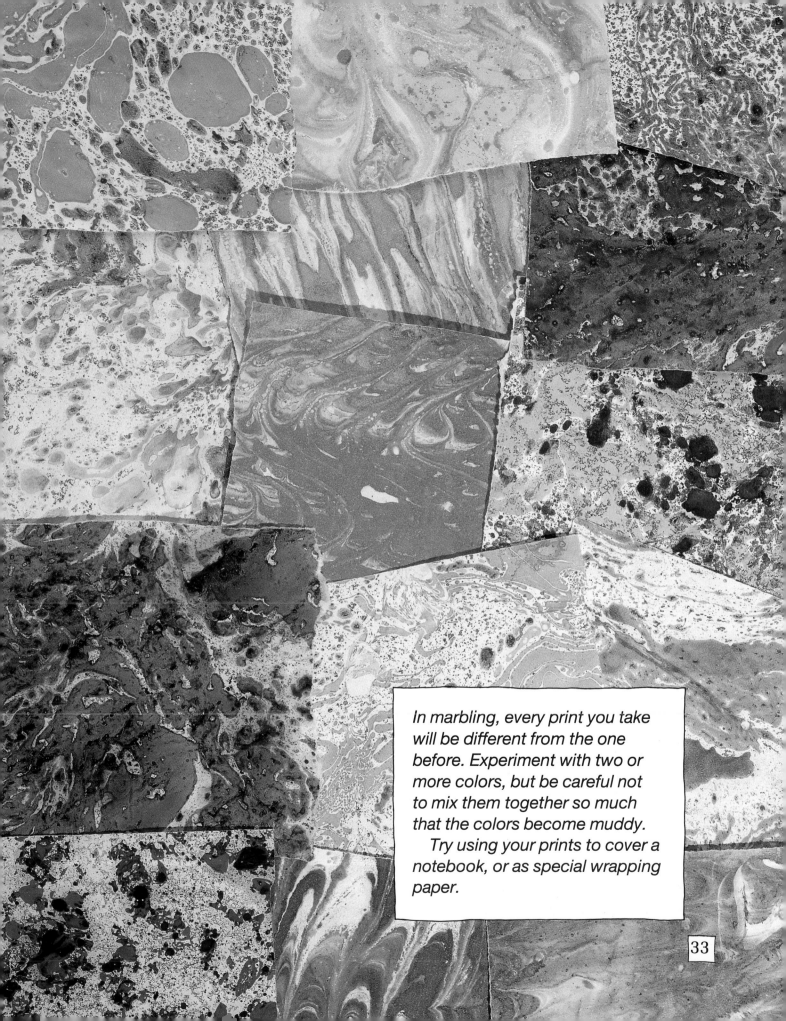

In marbling, every print you take will be different from the one before. Experiment with two or more colors, but be careful not to mix them together so much that the colors become muddy.

Try using your prints to cover a notebook, or as special wrapping paper.

FABRIC PRINTS

Fabric paints are sold in craft and hobby stores and are just as easy to print with as ordinary paints and inks. Use them to print on smooth materials — cotton is usually the best choice. Print T-shirts, sheets, pillowcases, socks or sneakers, or use scraps of material to make flags or banners.

1

Always wash and iron the fabric before you begin. If you're printing a T-shirt or a pillowcase, push a thick sheet of cardboard between the two layers.

2

Pin the item to a flat piece of cardboard, making sure that the surface is flat and smooth. Print as usual — for example, with a potato print.

3

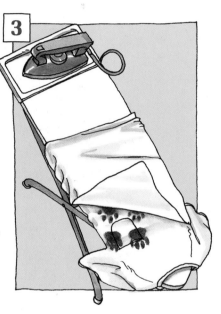

Most fabric paints need fixing with an iron — check the label, and ask an adult to help. Cover with a clean scrap of material, and iron over the top.

Right: The man-in-the-moon pillowcase was printed using masks (page 30). The spaces were stippled rather than sprayed, while the other pieces were held down with the fingers.

34

Above: Leaves were used to print the shirt (see page 12). The curtain was made from an old sheet stenciled with yellow stars (see page 28).

Left: The white T-shirt was decorated with a potato "paw" print (page 15).

CHINA PRINTS

Transform plain pieces of china into collector's items with ceramic paints! We used the oil-based type which fixes as it dries. You can also buy water-based paints, which need to be fired in an oven. Both types are waterproof.

Curved surfaces need flexible printers. A sponge square was glued to a small piece of wood to print a border on a plate, mug, and egg cup (shown in the photo).

The bathroom tiles were printed with shapes cut from cardboard (see page 16). A simple square can easily be used to build up a harlequin pattern using two colors.

The chicken design was stenciled, and the borders printed with sponge. The design on the seashore plate (below) was made by stippling over masks cut from cardboard.

Oil-based paints were used to print the china shown here. If you're using this type of paint, make sure you have plenty of mineral spirits to clean the brushes, and to wipe away any mistakes or spills.

USING PRINTS

Now that you know how to make prints, what are you going to do with them? Here are a few ideas.

Stationery

Print stationery for yourself or a friend — use plain writing paper and make a set of matching envelopes.

Printing is also perfect for mass-producing greeting cards, gift tags, and wrapping paper, and for taking the strain out of thank-you letters.

Decorating

Use prints to transform your room (furniture and floors will need a few coats of varnish to protect the paint). Try printing straight on walls, or make a frieze from paper.

You can also try doors, picture frames, lampshades, curtains, and quilt covers.

Parties

Paper tablecloths, cups, napkins, and place settings can all be printed with (waterproof!) paints and inks.

To print glitter on balloons, cut shapes out of foam and dip them in white glue. Press on the side of a blown-up balloon, and sprinkle with glitter.

Right: All the objects shown here have been decorated using printing methods from this book. To print on furniture, use household latex or gloss paints.

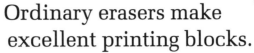

MORE IDEAS

Finally, here are a few more printing suggestions you might like to try...

Ordinary erasers make excellent printing blocks. Draw your design on one of the flat sides, and carefully cut around it with an art knife. You should be left with a raised printing surface (see potato prints, page 15).

Sets of playing cards and dominoes can be turned out quickly using prints. You could also design your own fake money...

Use the rubber blocks to print your own set of stamps! "Sew" the perforations with an unthreaded sewing machine...

Letter magnets can be used to print strong, clear letters and numbers (see right)...